I0020619

I. INTRODUCTION

A. PROBLEM STATEMENT

Smart cards used by Department of Defense (DOD) employees anticipate key length changes that make the performance time of smart cards untenable to users and card issuers in the future, based on the requirement that they be "strongly resistant to identity fraud, tampering, counterfeiting, and terrorist exploitation" per Homeland Security Presidential Directive 12 (DHS, 2004).

B. PURPOSE STATEMENT

The CAC (Common Access Card), the smart card used for standard identification and physical security access for thousands of DOD personnel, is set to undergo some changes due to higher security concerns. The Rivest-Shamir-Adleman (RSA) algorithm currently in use by the DOD is secure for now, but in the future, without significant key size increases, there is a risk of attack by hackers looking to gain access to information on the card. In comparison, the Elliptical Curve Cryptography (ECC) algorithm has been identified as a more secure and faster way of encrypting certificates with a lower bit size than the RSA algorithm.

The National Institute of Standards and Technology (NIST) recommends that in order to protect a symmetric key of 128 bits (Secret information as classified by NIST), the RSA key must be at least 3072 bits long to deter attackers, and this rate exponentially increases as the symmetric key size increases (The case for elliptic curve cryptography [The case], 2009). For Top Secret information, the number of bits required for RSA encryption (256 bits) is almost 30 times that of the (ECC) encryption algorithm (The case, 2009). This creates a situation where performance suffers as the size of the symmetric keys increase. The RSA algorithm size required to thwart would-be attackers is large enough to affect the speed of the transaction, which in turn would affect thousands of DOD workers. Closely related to the key size of different public key systems is the channel overhead required to perform key exchanges and digital signatures on a communications link (The case, 2009). The key size for the transaction is identical

1

to the number of bits being transferred. This scenario could have serious national security consequences for the war fighter who needs secure efficient and fast communication transfers.

The DOD launched a pilot program during the summer of 2014 using OPACITY software in conjunction with the ECC algorithm on mobile devices. Smart cards that use the ECC algorithm are now available to test performance measures with. This paper analyzes the performance of 14 standard encryption algorithms, including RSA and ECC, to compare and contrast the encryption timing of each using both contact and contactless connections, in hopes of providing physical evidence that, for the same level of security, ECC is the better algorithm to use. With data evidence, it will be possible to make a formal recommendation that DOD smart cards be migrated from using the RSA algorithm to the ECC algorithm.

This paper will define the ECC algorithm and compare the number of bits required for effective and efficient security to the currently used RSA algorithm. A case study focusing on OPACITY software will be described, and testing will be conducted on smart cards. Testing for this thesis will include taking a measure of on-card performance of 14 encryption algorithms, differentiated by both algorithm and bytes, and measured in groups by iteration. Additionally, more comprehensive testing of end-to-end ECC performance across DOD networks will be included, recording comparisons of performance between contact readers, desktop contactless readers, and mobile NFC devices. Standard deviations will be calculated to identify any data collected that falls outside the norm. Graphs will be designed to display the different algorithms and their performance compared to the others. Lastly, a potential DOD move from RSA to ECC algorithms will be analyzed for risk and mitigating factors. The following outline briefly describes each chapter of the thesis.

1. Comparative Analysis of ECC versus RSA Algorithms

The ECC cryptography algorithm requires significantly fewer bits to protect the same sized symmetric key as the RSA cryptography algorithm. The second chapter of this thesis will contrast and compare in laymen's terms the ECC and RSA cryptography algorithms, focusing on the improvements that can be made by implementing ECC on the smart card.

2. Open Protocol for Access Control Identification and Ticketing with privacY Case Study

The third chapter will highlight a case study being tested at the Defense Manpower Data Center (DMDC) in Seaside, CA, focusing on Open Protocol for Access Control Identification and Ticketing with privacY (OPACITY), a protocol created for secure contactless communications using smart cards. The underlying technology will be stipulated but real-world data will be provided to illustrate the functionalities of the protocol enabling secure digitally signed and encrypted emails using Near Field Communication (NFC) contactless smart cards. Providing secure communications over mobile phone technologies is a high-level initiative for the DOD across the board as it will enable vetted defense users to communicate with one another using Public Key Infrastructure (PKI) technology on their smart phones in a secure, reliable, and timely manner.

3. Card Testing and Algorithm Performance Comparison

The fourth chapter will delve into the meat of the thesis, describing a java program written to test DOD CAC cards that have ECC algorithms implemented. Test data will be analyzed for performance measurements such as average key generation times and key generation probability distributions to compare RSA results with the ECC results now available in this research. The top three categories of this testing are signing digital certificates, encrypting and decrypting messages.

4. Risk and Mitigation Analysis for Move from RSA to ECC Algorithm

The last chapter will provide updated requirements and deadlines across the DOD for the latest encryption and mobile technology standards. Risks and possible risk mitigation will be discussed for the DOD migration from RSA technology to ECC technology, as all currently issued CAC cards would need to be re-issued with the new

CAC hardware. This migration will likely be slow and difficult so the goal will be to minimize the impact of changes on users.

II. COMPARATIVE ANALYSIS OF ECC VERSUS RSA ALGORITHM

A. PROBLEMS OF THE RIVEST-SHAMIR-ADLEMAN CRYPTOGRAPHIC ALGORITHM

Smart cards—mini computer systems—are being used around the world today to complete millions of transactions, including transaction types such as identification, financial (electronic wallets), transport, and even application processing. There is increased need for security as sensitive military, commercial and private data increasingly becomes transmitted wirelessly…which translates into more sophisticated encryption algorithms which add to additional hardware, power and time requirements (Owor, Dajani, Okonkwo, & Hamilton, 2007). Digital signatures and encryption are the two most important uses of smart cards within the DOD, which enables the cards to be Personal Identity Verification (PIV) cards per the National Institute of Standards and Technology (NIST). The PIV standards laid out in Federal Information Processing Standard (FIPS) 201 set requirements for federal employees and contractors accessing information systems (Department of Commerce, 2013).

Smart cards within the DOD are primarily used as security tokens to establish proof of identity, through verification of certifications stored on the smart card using encryption algorithms. Every cryptosystem relies upon what is hoped to be an unsolvable mathematical problem, and this is the encryption algorithm that is used. It is imperative that encryption algorithms do not add an overbearing cost in terms of time, power and weight to the design of these systems (Owor et al., 2007). A public key infrastructure (PKI) issues encrypted digital certificates to users which are stored on the smart card itself, and a pair of asymmetric keys are generated by an encryption algorithm every time the certificates need to be accessed. An asymmetric key pair is used since it establishes a pair for every user needed on the smart card rather than multiple pairs of key sets like a symmetric key. The encryption algorithm should provide the highest possible level of encryption security at the lowest possible cost in terms of the size of the encryption key, the number of operations and the unit time of encryption (Owor et al., 2007). The length of a key, in bits, for a conventional encryption algorithm is a common measure of security (The case, 2009).

Currently, the RSA cryptographic algorithm is being used to verify identity certifications on smart cards for the DOD. This algorithm was one of the first widely accepted secure methods of private key encryption in use for data transmission. The premise of the algorithm is that a public and private key is generated by the algorithm. The public key is generated to encrypt the data and the private key is generated to decrypt the data. The RSA algorithm problem rests on determining what the prime numbers being used are, the "factoring problem." The product of these prime numbers plus an additional random value is what makes up the public key. The key set is generated by the RSA algorithm every time the card is accessed by the user in order to determine the identity of the user by verifying the encrypted digital certificate of that user.

The key set is generated by using the following algorithm (al Hasib & Haque, 2008):

1. Select two large prime numbers p and q (e.g. 1024 bits each) such that p 6=q.
2. Compute modulus n = p.q
3. Calculate totient, '(n) = (p-1).(q-1)
4. Choose an integer (public exponent) e, 1 ¡ e ¡ '(n), such that gcd(e, '(n)) = 1.
5. Compute the secret exponent d, 1 ¡ d ¡ '(n), such that d:e _1 (mod n).
6. The public key is (n, e)
7. And the private key is (n, d).

The main drawback of RSA is its efficiency, in particular for some devices with limited computing power such as smart cards (Nassr, Bahig, Bhery & Daoud, 2008). RSA keys being used in smart cards had a length of 1024 bits a few years ago. This is no longer recommended since a short RSA key can be discovered through security attacks such as a brute force attack or mathematical attack. Instead, a 2048 bit length is now used in CAC and PIV cards. The number of values that must be tried…with a brute force attack…doubles with each bit added to the key length (Owor et al., 2007), making the algorithm more difficult to break; however, the larger key will make the encryption and decryption process a little slow as it will require greater computations in key generation as well as in encryption/decryption algorithm (al Hasib & Haque, 2008). The longer the key length required the slower the performance for the key generation. It is this decrease in efficiency that makes increasing the bit length of the RSA algorithm an untenable solution to increase the security of smart cards for users in the DOD who must access digital certificates repeatedly throughout the work day.

B. BENEFITS OF THE ELLIPTIC CURVE CRYPTOSYSTEM

The Elliptic Curve Cryptosystem is an improvement on RSA because it uses an elliptic curve algorithm that reduces the amount of bits required for the same level of security. This is becoming increasingly important due to the higher level of threats from hacking technologies. Gupta stated that an Elliptical curve may be defined as an equation of the form ay2 + bxy = cx3 + dx2 + ex + f, where a, b, c, d, e, f, x and y are for cryptographic purposes restricted to each belong to a finite field i.e., a, b, c, d, e, f, x and y are each chosen from a distinct set of integral values as cited in Owor et al., 2007. The ECC relies upon the difficulty of the Elliptic Curve Discrete Logarithm Problem (ECDLP) (Owor et al., 2007) as its unsolvable mathematical problem. NIST has published the Digital Signature Standard (DSS), (FIPS 186–4), which standardizes the Elliptic Curve Digital Signature Algorithm (ECDSA) and recommends fifteen sets of elliptic curve domain parameters to be used in ECC cryptosystems. The NSA has endorsed the use of ECC in its Suite B1 set of algorithms, which have been deemed secure for Top Secret, Secret, and Sensitive but Unclassified information.

ECC devices "smaller key sizes result in smaller system parameters, smaller public-key signatures, bandwidth savings, faster implementations, lower power requirements, and smaller hardware processors" (Chatterjee & Gupta, 2009). The digital signatures created by the algorithm are smaller since they are more computationally efficient. They will require less overhead to transmit as well. For example, the 224 bit ECC key provides the same amount of security as a 2048 bit RSA key. This makes ECC the perfect choice for a space limited device such as the smart card where minimizing power and energy consumption is crucial. With ECC, the time needed to generate a key pair is so short that even a device with the very limited computing power of a smart card can generate the key pair, provided a good random number generator is available (Chatterjee & Gupta, 2009). The ECC algorithm will grow in usage as information becomes more and more secure. Figure 1 demonstrates the difference in key sizes between an RSA key and an ECC key, as well as the ratio of cost of the Diffie-Hellman Key size to the ECC key size.

Photo Removed Due to Copyright Restrictions

Figure 1.   NIST Recommended Key Sizes and Relative Computation Costs.
(after "The case for elliptic curve cryptography," 2009).

It is important to remember that the speed of the cryptography computing process does take its toll in a financial sense as well, when you consider that over 1.5 million transactions are logged daily (US DOD CAC, 2010). The biggest performance difference is when the smart card has to generate a public/private key pair. The ECC and RSA Algorithm Performance Comparison (key pair generation), presented in Figure 14 in Section IV of this paper, showed that the RSA algorithm at 2048 bits was 46 times computationally slower than the ECC algorithm at the same number of bits. Each RSA key generation took approximately 38 seconds while each ECC key generation took less than one second. To translate this financially, for each key pair generation taking approximately 38 seconds for an employee making $30/hour would cost: 0.63 minutes wait time per person per transaction x $0.50/minute estimated labor cost ($30/hour). For a Verifying Official(VO) working at a Real-Time Automated Personnel Identification System (RAPIDS) site distributing cards to a DOD employee (2 users) each RSA card would cost $0.32 more than an ECC card simply based on the time it takes to generate the key pair. If 500 cards a day are produced at a Card Issuance Facility (CIF) it would take five hours to generate the key process on the cards with the RSA algorithm while the same number of cards with the ECC algorithm could be produced in less than 10 minutes. For every 500 cards issued, RSA costs will be over twice as much as ECC costs, and employees will not be able to produce as many cards. This example is a fraction of actual card transactions occurring within the DOD, so the end total loss in wait time for DOD employees is not trivial.

THIS PAGE INTENTIONALLY LEFT BLANK

III. OPACITY CASE STUDY

A. MOBILE DEVICE SMART CARD LIMITATIONS

The Department of Defense is the nation's largest employer, currently employing over two million people: 1.4 million active duty military, 718,000 civilian employees, and 1.1 million National Guard and Reserve military (Figure 2). There are over 5000 sites or installations where DOD employees work all over the world.

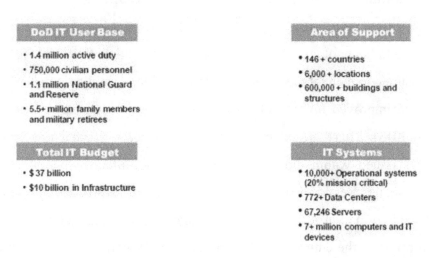

Figure 2.   DOD IT infrastructure characteristics (from Information Technology (IT) Enterprise Strategy and Roadmap, 2011.).

The mission of the DOD is to protect the security of the United States of America, and all of the employees of the DOD require Common Access Cards (CAC) in order to perform their work securely and access working sites securely using the certifications stored on the smart cards as a means of PIV authentication. The majority of DOD sites today (whether physical access sites or websites on the Internet) require digital certification upon logon, which requires the CAC card. The certifications on the CAC card are accessed hundreds of times per working day per employee, so with a time estimate of 6–8 seconds per access multiplied by ~100 times a day per employee, there is a significant amount of time being used on CAC transactions. Currently, employees within the DOD use the Microsoft Outlook mail client in order to send digitally signed and encrypted emails to and from one another. This mail client can be accessed through a web browser but encrypted and digitally signed documents are not enabled unless a CAC reader is also connected to the device in question in order to access the certificates on the CAC itself.

According to IDC (Market Analysis: Worldwide Mobile Enterprise Security Software 2012–2016 Forecast and Analysis), mobile identity and access management is expected to grow by 27.6 percent between 2010 and 2016 (Effective identity and access management in a mobile world, n.d.). There is significant growth in mobile communications within the United States, and within the DOD, the Chairman of the Joint Chiefs of Staff's Capstone Concept for Joint Operations: Joint Force 2020, Reference (b), recognizes mobile technology as a key capability enabler for joint force combat operations; secure commercial mobile applications are increasingly viewed as essential to innovations and improved mission effectiveness across a wide range of DOD mission areas (Takia, 2013). There are at least 11,000 Government Funded Equipment (GFE) mobile phones issued within the Marine Corps services alone (FICAM Mobile Pilot Solution Case Studies Version 1.0, personal communication, April, 2014). Achieving and maintaining the information advantage as a critical element of national power requires the concentrated effort of the entire DOD to provide an information environment optimized for the warfighter and effective for all echelons, from the tactical edge to the strategic core (Information Technology (IT) Enterprise Strategy and Roadmap, 2011).

"A mobile device… is a portable computing device that: (i) has a small form factor such that it can easily be carried by a single individual; (ii) is designed to operate without a physical connection (e.g., wirelessly transmit or receive information); (iii) possesses local, non-removable or removable data storage; and (iv) includes a self-contained power source…but mobile devices lack the integrated smart card readers found in laptop and desktop computers and require separate card readers attached to devices to provide authentication services from the device" (Federal Information Security Management Act (FISMA), Public Law (P.L.) 107–347, 2014). Mobile devices are generally too small to integrate smart card readers into the device itself, requiring alternative approaches for communicating between the PIV Card and the mobile device

(FISMA, Public Law (P.L.) 107–347, 2014). Smart card technology is present in almost all mobile devices, either on the SIM card or through another secure element like a Secure Digital (SD) card.

B. DOD PROOF OF CONCEPT

The DOD has sponsored development of the Open Protocol for Access Control, Identification, and Ticketing with privacy (OPACITY), which is a Diffie-Hellman-based key exchange protocol to establish secure channels in contactless environments. The protocol has been registered as an ISO/IEC 24727–6 authentication protocol and is specified in the draft ANSI 504–1 national standard (GICS) (Dagdelen, Fischlin, Gagliardoni, Marson, Mittelbach, & Onete, 2013). It is compliant with the recommendation by the National Institute of Standards and Technology (NIST) in the "Recommendation for Pair-Wise Key Establishment Schemes Using Discrete Logarithm Cryptography" publication 800–56Ar2, 2013, as well as the National Security Agency's (NSA) Suite B Cryptography standards. The Opacity software uniquely and securely identifies each cardholder over a contactless interface using the PKI certificates, which are hard to reproduce. Opacity uses two key exchange protocols: Zero Key Management (ZKM) and Full Secrecy (FS). The ZKM protocol only ensures the identity of the cardholder and does not require maintaining registered public keys. The FS protocol will require mutual authentication and is a secure way to protect both the identities of the communicating parties as well as the message in relay itself which is encrypted using ECC. OPACITY has been targeted for use in many ways. Some examples of possible OPACITY use cases are shown in Figure 3.

Photo Removed Due to Copyright Restricitons

Figure 3.   OPACITY USE CASES. (from ACTIVIDENTITY: The Open
Protocol for Access Control Identification and Ticketing with PrivacY
For Secure Contactless Transactions and Enabling Logical and
Physical Access [Powerpoint] (n.d.). Retrieved August 2014.

OPACITY contains a Secure Authentication Module (SAM) that is similar to the Hardware Security Module (HSM) within a smart card (Figure 4). The SAM contains a private key and root public keys and helps to establish sessions once the application in question has asked for authentication from the smart card. Both the SAM and the smart card will generate keys that will be matched and authentication will be granted if the match is successful.

Photo Removed Due to Copyright Restricitons

Figure 4.   OPACITY simple command flow. (after ACTIVIDENTITY: The
Open Protocol for Access Control Identification and Ticketing with
PrivacY For Secure Contactless Transactions and Enabling Logical
and Physical Access [PowerPoint] n.d. Retrieved August 2014.

14

The primary goal of the OPACITY Proof of Concept (POC) at DMDC was to demonstrate secure PKI transactions using smart cards over a Near Field Communication (NFC) contactless interface. There were also four main objectives working toward this goal (HID Professional Services Document NFC Mobile PoC Integration Test Report, personal communication, March 31, 2014)

:

- To demonstrate the feasibility of securing the NFC contactless interface in a mobile environment simply by holding an OPACITY-enabled smartcard to the back of the phone—without a Bluetooth smartcard sled reader, a connected reader or alternate secure element such as a secure microSD.
- To demonstrate the business value of OPACITY to enforce the Government mobility mandates for mobile devices (alignment with ANSI 504 / GICS part 1 and FIPS 201–2: Secure Contact interface).
- To identify the improvements and/or adjustments needed in the infrastructure to promote the use of mobile devices by Government employees.
- To assess any technology limitations in order to use existing NFC-enabled smart phones to operate with new generations of the CAC. The purpose is also to gather requirements for the upcoming generation of cards and smart phones to support above use cases

These objectives fulfilled the directive of the DOD Identify Council to both use PKI credentials on the smart card while securing the mobile work environment. Since an NFC-enabled mobile device can interact with a PIV Card over its contactless antenna at a very close range, the mobile device can use the keys on the PIV Card without a physical connection (FISMA, Public Law (P.L.) 107–347). It still uses a two-factor challenge/response system that asks for a pin and responds to the request. The technology chosen must also incorporate Public-Key Cryptography Standards (PKSC) #11 which deals with cryptographic tokens (i.e., the certificates existing on the smart card). Requirements for the pilot project were outlined in the original scope proof of concept document (HID Professional Services Document NFC Mobile PoC Integration Test Report, personal communication, March 31, 2014):

- Requirement 1: The mobile email client shall use the OPACITY protocol to authenticate the user and use Secure Messaging to secure the CAC contactless interface for PKI transactions

- Requirement 2: The PoC solution shall support the email signing and email decryption use cases
- Requirement 3: The email client application should enforce the cardholders authentication to the mobile email client using the CAC
- Requirement 4: The PoC shall be conducted on an external facing infrastructure. This intention of this PoC is not only to demonstrate the use of the mobile email application using the CAC, but to use the solution in a real-world environment to assess real-world obstacles or ease of use. Hence, the PoC email infrastructure must be accessible via the NIPRNet rather than only within a closed lab environment.
- Requirement 5: The PoC solution shall support up to 40 participants
- Requirement 6: The evaluation cards issued to participants shall use fictitious user information to avoid exposing any Personally Identifiable information
- Requirement 7: The email transactions shall utilize DISA test certificates. The CAC-Like cards will request the ID, PIV authentication, email and signing certificates from the DISA test Certificate Authority.
- Requirement 8: The PoC shall only use CAC-Like test cards encoded with the DOD CAC+PIV EP Data Model
- Requirement 9: The PoC Shall limit the use cases to PKI operations. The card surface printing shall clearly identify the card as a sample card for the DMDC Mobile NFC Proof of Concept and must not resemble the FIPS 201–1 card surface requirements.
- Requirement 10: The PoC Shall limit the use cases to PKI operations. The PoC use cases do not encompass the use of the CAC Demographic data or biometric data. Therefore, the PoC card personalization must include specific test data:
- Requirement 11: The PoC shall support specific mobile phone devices
- Requirement 12: The PoC shall support specific card platforms which is considered proprietary information and will not be shared in this thesis.

DMDC partners with HID for the PoC cards: creation, pin reset, termination and reissue. The cards used in the POC project were generated by HID since the current CAC cards at DMDC do not support a specific applet that was still in development and under review by NIST. HID partners with Good for Government Technology to provide both a commercial secure email client and a mobile device manager (MDM) as the interface used to test out the smart card certifications, both for the Good enterprise servers, the ActivId application, and the email client. A breakdown of roles and responsibilities per organization for the PoC is presented in Figure 5.

Photo Removed Due to Copyright Restricitons

Figure 5.   Integration Summary, from HID Professional Services Document NFC Mobile PoC Integration Test Report, personal communication, March 31, 2014

Good Technology is promoting its enterprise data and device management system used to secure access to email through certificate-based authentication Secure/Multipurpose Internet Mail Extensions (S/MIME). The software provides a seamless interface on different device platforms including Android, iOS, and Windows. Good Technology supports all legacy smart cards or the users can choose to use a MicroSD card within their mobile phones as the primary credential. Following is an example of the different features available from Good Technology (Figure 6).

Photo Removed Due to Copyright Restricitons

Figure 6.   Management and Control Features from Good for Enterprise Data Sheet [Brochure]. (n.d). Retrieved August 2014 from https://media.good.com/documents/ds-good-for-enterprise.pdf

The Defense Manpower Data Center (DMDC) received several Samsung and Galaxy phones (Android) from different mobile phone carriers to use in the test pilot. Specially configured test CACs and test DOD PKI certificates were used in conjunction with the phones to test specific use cases. These test CACs, provided by card manufacturers, allowed encrypted PKI transactions over contactless interfaces. The Proof of Concept cards are non-FIPS versions of the next generation of card platforms. These DMDC-selected cards support Elliptic Curve Cryptography used by the OPACITY protocol and support NFC used to communicate with the mobile device (HID Professional Services Document NFC Mobile PoC Integration Test Report, personal communication, March 31, 2014). DMDC provided the fictitious data that was used to identify the smart cards being used during the testing, plus the test certificates provided by DISA. The certificates include: ID certificate, Email Signing Certificate, Email Encryption Certificate, and the PIV Authentication Certificate., although only the email certificates were tested. Basically, the testers had to hold an OPACITY-enabled smart card to the back of the mobile device, authenticate into the MDM, and secure the existing email application with PKI certificates on the CAC to digitally sign, encrypt, and decrypt email contactlessly (see Figure 7). It was necessary to do this without a connected card reader or secure microSD within the mobile device. The transaction between the card and the device is encrypted using an ANSI 504 OPACITY ZKM secure channel. This Diffie-Hellman Elliptic Curve Cryptography is a non-proprietary way to encrypt the contactless channel of the CAC.

Photo Removed Due to Copyright Restricitons

Figure 7.   NFC-Enabled Mobile Phone Used as a Reader (Mobile devices and identity applications [Publication] September 2012. Retrieved March 2015)

DMDC employees were tasked with testing the phones for five specific use cases. The use cases consisted of the following:

- User Authentication
- Send and receive Signed email, with and without attachments
- Send and Receive Encrypted email, with and without attachments
- Send and Receive both Signed/Encrypted email, with and without attachments
- Usability Testing (Loss of NFC Session)

The user must be able to authenticate to the Good application in five seconds or less (a timely manner) by responding to the prompt for credentials with the user's pin, and receiving an acknowledgment that the authentication requirements have been satisfied. In order to send a signed and/or encrypted email the user must establish a secure session and the application establishes the hashed data to be signed by the user's email signing key on the PoC card. In order to receive a signed email the process is reversed: the application is able to decrypt the provided hash and verify it matches the email client's calculated hash. This process is duplicated for emails that contain attachments. The user also should verify that the time taken to sign and/or encrypt an email is a reasonable amount of time, within a few seconds. A major part of the usability testing concerned the success or failure rate of the NFC connection. Users documented how difficult it might have been to determine the correct location of the connection between the smart card and the NFC connection, and the success and failure rate of that connection especially during specific tasks such as encrypting an email. Users were also asked whether or not they might have preferred a protective case that correctly positioned the card upon the NFC antenna, however, since the antenna location is in different locations for different phones this would be a difficult prospect. An illustration of the proper connection area for a Samsung Galaxy 3 is shown in Figure 8.

Photo Removed Due to Copyright Restricitons

Figure 8.   Using contactless cards with NFC-enabled devices (HID
TECHNICAL NOTE Document Version 1.1: Using Contactless
Cards with NFC-Enabled Devices, personal communication, March
2014)

The OPACITY pilot at DMDC was considered a success. All stakeholders involved (DMDC, HID Global, and Good Technologies) worked together on the objectives and outcomes and demonstrated effective team participation. All testers indicated that the contactless connection when working properly is the most convenient and cost effective way to authenticate to a mobile device. Testers provided valuable feedback on the testing experience that can be used to improve the process in the future. A timing delay was discovered in a specific card model and the vendor was made aware of it in order to make necessary changes. A bug in manufactured NFC readers was also discovered and that information was made available to the vendor for correction. Specific points gained from testing included:

- Smart card RF Signal strength needs improvement and different card vendors should standardize for consistent RF strength
- NFC reader signal strength on mobile phones needs improvement as well as a standardized position for the NFC connection; addition of smart card testing at manufacturer level needs to occur
- Smart card response time and performance must be improved, ideally between 300–500 ms per transaction
- Smart card vendors should work on non-proprietary solutions that mesh with standards being developed; gov't should identify their needs and work with vendors to incorporate those needs when possible

THIS PAGE INTENTIONALLY LEFT BLANK

IV. CARD TESTING AND ALGORITHM PERFORMANCE COMPARISON

This portion of the paper focuses on the testing of smart cards to compare the key generation time for different algorithms. The key generation time is important in terms of the OPACITY test pilot because the NFC connection over a mobile phone must be fast enough to enable Department of Defense employees to sign and encrypt emails in a reasonable amount of time, ideally 3/10–5/10 of a second per transaction. Three different types of cards by manufacturer were used which will be identified by Card 1, Card 2, and Card 3. Four different types of algorithms were used: SHA, AES, RSA, and ECC. Some of the tests focused on key generation, key computation, and key agreement. In addition, different key lengths for each algorithm were also used to track the operation time for each length. Lastly, each algorithm was tested for three different numbers of iterations in order to determine whether the number of iterations increased the time taken to complete the specific transaction.

Three specific operations were tested: compute, key generation, and key agreement. Compute simply means performing the standard algorithm identified in each test. Key generation is the process of creating a public and private key pair. The encryption key is public and the decryption key is private. The key agreement test consists of the basic Hellman-Diffie test: two users can exchange keys with one another by establishing a shared secret key. The compute test was performed on the Secure Hash Algorithm (SHA) and Advanced Encryption Standard (AES) algorithms. The key generation test was performed on the RSA and ECC algorithms. The key agreement test was only performed on the ECC algorithm.

This particular set of tests was run on a contactless interface (having the smart card connect with the smart card reader wirelessly using the RF signal). All of the testing was done using a T=1 protocol which means that each APDU transaction has the capability to send a command and receive data within one transaction. The time involved in setting up the command with just the algorithms was isolated in order to subtract it out from the timing of the actual operations being performed on each algorithm. Results were

23

returned in seconds, milliseconds, and microseconds. All results were converted to microseconds since it was the smallest common unit of return. The types of operations, algorithms, and bit lengths tested are identified in Table 1.

OPERATION	ALGORITHM	BIT LENGTH
Compute	SHA	1
		256
		384
	AES	128
		192
		256
Generate	RSA	1024
		2048
	ECC	224
		256
		384
Key Agreement		224
		256
		384

Table 1.   Operation, algorithm, and bit length testing

Demonstrating the value of testing was a challenge for several reasons. Different capabilities existed on the three different types of cards. Comparisons between all cards could not be done since different operations, algorithms, and bit lengths were available only on certain cards. First, not all cards could support the same algorithms. For instance, Card 2 did not contain the RSA algorithm or the SHA and ECC bit length 384 algorithms so the results were empty for that set of tests. Another example: Card 1 came back with 'UNKNOWN' results for the ECC Key Agreement operation which indicates that the test failed but left no conclusion as to what might have gone wrong. The cards were tested at 300, 1000, and 5000 iterations and the results were all similar in scope between the three different iterations. In general, the operation timing decreased as the number of iterations increased because the command generation time (subtracted from the operation timing) had less of an effect on a higher number of iterations. Figure 9 shows (in cards 1, 2, and 3) that the operation length decreased with each set of iterations.

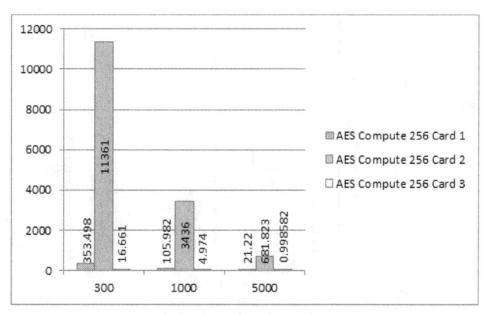

Figure 9.   Timing decreases as number of iterations increases

A.   PERFORMANCE COMPARISON OF THREE CARD TYPES

Each following section will focus on a specific algorithm tested at different bit lengths. Not all bit lengths are supported by all card algorithms. Charts will show visual representation of the results of each test set.

1.   AES Algorithm

Figure 10 shows the comparison between the three different card types for the computation of the AES algorithm tested at bit lengths of 128, 192, and 256. Card 2 took significantly more time than Cards 1 and 3. This type of testing is especially beneficial for organizations such as DMDC in order to determine which card type will best fulfill requirements of specific initiatives.

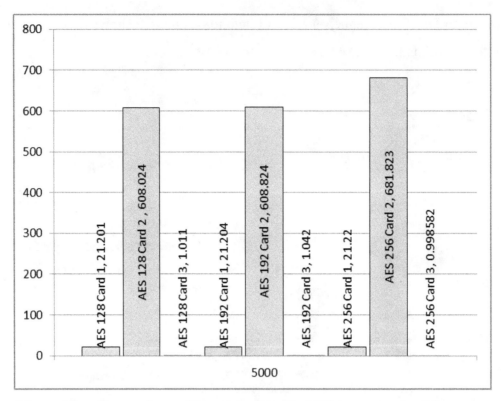

Figure 10.   Comparison of 3 card types with AES compute algorithm

2.   SHA Algorithm

Figure 11 shows the same type of card comparison but compares the computation of the SHA algorithm instead. For the Block 1 and 256 bit lengths, Card 2 takes longer to compute the same algorithm. Card 2 does not support the 384 bit length test so no results were returned for that test.

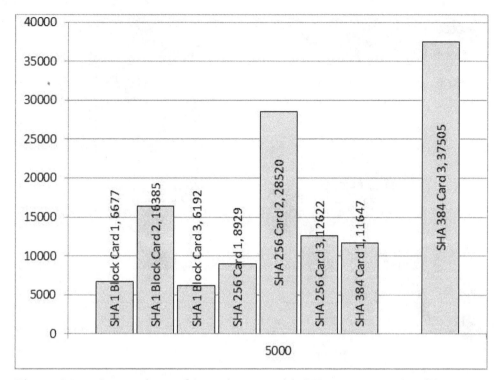

Figure 11.   Comparison of 3 card types with SHA compute algorithm

3.   ECC Algorithm

Figure 12 is a comparison of the key generation process on three different types of cards using ECC. The bit length of 384 is not supported on Card 2 so that test result is missing but card 2 has the slowest performance on all other supported bit lengths. Card 1 has the fastest performance for all tested bit lengths.

27

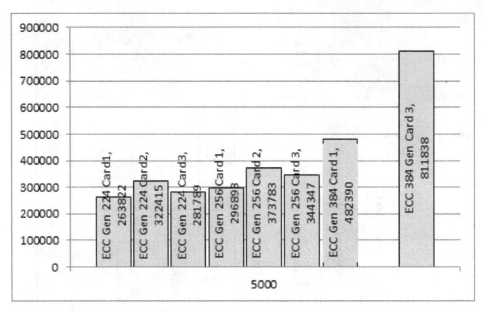

Figure 12. Comparison of key generation of 3 card types with ECC compute
algorithm

Figure 13 is a comparison of the key agreement process on three different types of
cards using ECC. Card 1 did not support this algorithm at all, and Card 2 only supported
the algorithm for 224 and 256 bit lengths. Card 3 was the only card that supported this
algorithm at the 384 bit length, so if this level of security was needed for a specific
process, then this type of card would be the only available card to work with.

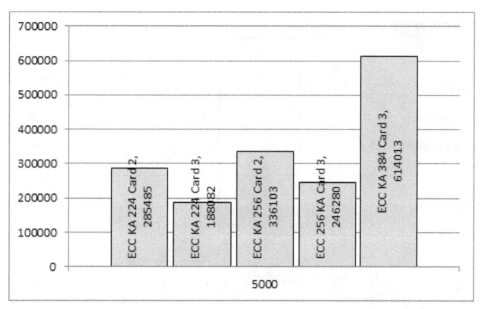

Figure 13.   Comparison of key agreement. 3 card types with ECC compute algorithm

4.   ECC and RSA Algorithm Performance Comparison

Figure 14 contains the most important results in terms of the pilot project identified in this paper. It compares the speed of key generation using the RSA algorithm against the speed of key generation using the ECC algorithm at equivalent bit lengths. According to data generated by NIST, the performance cost of using the RSA algorithm is six times higher than that of using the ECC algorithm at the same bit length. This means that in order to provide the same level of security as the ECC algorithm, the RSA algorithm would take six times as long to generate keys. This was corroborated by the test performed on available cards for this research. Cards 1 and 2 did not support testing the RSA algorithm for key generation at 2048 bytes. The only key generation comparison that could be made at an equivalent bit length between RSA and ECC with provided card materials was using Card 3. It took the RSA algorithm approximately 46 times longer to generate the key than it did the ECC algorithm.

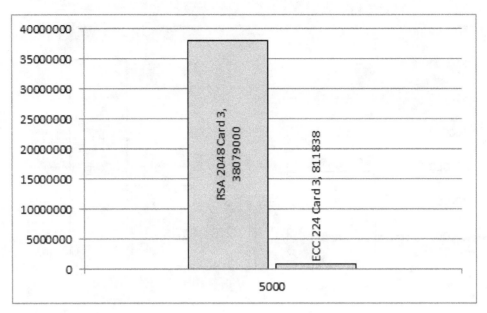

Figure 14.   Comparison of RSA to ECC compute algorithm

V. RISK AND MITIGATION ANALYSIS FOR MOVE FROM RSA TO ECC ALGORITHM

According to the DOD Mobile Device Strategy, "successful execution…" of an implementation plan "relies on the collaboration and cooperation of all DOD components and on partnerships with federal, intelligence, academia, and commercial communities," but that it is necessary to keep the DOD workforce "relevant in an era when information and cyberspace play a critical role in mission success" (DOD, 2014). A primary goal of the Mobile Device Strategy is to "Institute Mobile Device Policies and Standards," which encompasses the usage of commercial products in a timely manner as well as a system that can securely manage them in addition to education for mobile device users.

DOD must establish a mobile device security architecture which includes the "Public Key Infrastructure security, access, and identification controls at the network, device, and application levels" (DOD, 2014). The cryptographic implementation (ECC algorithm) should follow the recommendations of NSA/NIST in all categories. In addition, conforming to standards of the Common Criteria for Information Technology Security Evaluation (CC), an international standard for computer security assurances, is advisable.

The implementation must be enterprise-wide but must also support executive and tactical or battlefield mission critical agendas. Unfortunately, the lengthy certification processes required for most United States government makes adoption of any new technologies a slow and challenging undertaking. The following standards need to be taken into consideration when implementing changes to any government issued card process: Federal Information Processing Standard (FIPS 201, FIPS 140), NIST Recommendation (i.e., NIST SP800–63–1, SP 800–157). Government IT departments will have to configure and manage the new technology in terms of mobile authentication. This will require extensive user training and must conform to the existing smart card regulations.

Coordination with third-party vendors is a critical factor. Card vendors must not create proprietary solutions but must instead focus on conforming to U.S. government and ANSI standards. Card manufacturers must be able to provide these in the quantity desired. Once the new algorithm has been integrated into the smart cards, the smart cards will be implemented into the current processes for dispensing cards to users. In addition, the administration will have to determine whether or not users can Bring Your Own Device (BYOB) or use only Government Funded Equipment (GFE). Limiting devices to GFE allows the agency to more closely manage the device and application usage than they would be able to for bring your own device (BYOD) [Mobile Pilot Solution Case Studies Version 1.0], personal communication, April, 2014]. Either way, training will need to be provided in order to use mobile device certificate signing and encryption. This training should be done in a general application or demonstration.

The protection of privacy is a huge initiative within the DOD. The CAC contains a variety of Personally Identifiable Information (PII) which must be protected from unauthorized access (Preliminary Confidentiality Impact Level Analysis–version 0 6, personal communication, April 2014). Therefore, consideration of the protection of this information has to be paramount in the implementation of accessing CACs through a mobile device. The DOD has applied the assessment model described in NIST SP 800–122 to determine a Preliminary Confidentiality Impact Level Assessment of the PII and linked and linkable data contained in the chip on the PIV card in the context of a Contactless Secure Messaging solution. This includes information in the x.509 certificate, the Card Holder Unique Identifier, and possibly biometrics data and personal data. The biometrics data is especially considered high importance since it is not easily accessed elsewhere. This makes the features available on the cards extremely critical—the card manufacturers must take responsibility to remove any and all unused features on the card in order to avoid possible pathways to manipulate and extract card content. In addition, users should be required to have CAC cards contained within radio frequency shields so that contactless interference cannot occur.

One concern that was addressed is the possibility of "sniffing" vulnerabilities through the contactless interface, since contactless transactions have not been used before but would be required in the mobile scenario. The information available for sniffing on the card, which includes attributes such as different name types and email addresses are

32

easily obtained through other means than the CAC card, so are not deemed a significant privacy risk. A secure messaging (SM) channel that implements digital signatures, enforcing integrity of information, is used to access the objects on the contactless interface. SM requires that the card be within a specific distance from the reader in order to power the card. Electromagnetic opaque sleeves can also be used to mitigate the risk, and the combination of these three factors actually entails less risk than the contact reader interface, since contactless transaction times are much shorter than those of a card sitting within the reader for an unspecified amount of time. In addition, a pairing code is being proposed that would require a six digit pin be entered prior to any certificates being accessed on the card. The pairing code would 'pair' a reader and a card together which would prevent any other rogue devices from 'skimming' information off of the card. If a pairing code is added to the process then DOD will incur significant additional costs and development time to add this feature. These recommendations must be evaluated prior to final implementation of CAC mobile access.

Separate mobile pilots were also executed by the Defense Information Systems Agency (DISA), the U.S. Marine Corps (USMC), and the U.S. Department of Agriculture (USDA). A gap analysis was done as an overview for mobile technology and technical, policy, and marketplace gaps were identified. Technical gaps included the control of personal information on mobile devices (especially in terms of legal liability), the lack of standardization for PIV technologies (especially in terms of security), and the lack of available Certificate Authorities (CA) to handle the software certificates needed to access mobile devices. Policy gaps included policy questions regarding two-factor authentication requirements by the Office of Management and Budget (OMB), questions of whether the PIV certificates meet requirements for Level of Assurance (LOA) 4 authentication, and whether or not certificate solutions align with the upcoming NIST SP 800–157. Marketplace gaps included the lack of mobile device and application management solutions (especially for Bring Your Own Device (BYOD) programs), lack of federally approved secure mobile device solutions, lack of applications that support the use of PIV credentials, and lack of vetting solutions for new and updated application vetting. Recommendations were made to mitigate the technical, policy, and marketplace gaps but these would require a concerted effort between government agencies, mobile device manufacturers, hardware component developers, service providers, and third-party vendors.

DISA has been incorporating mobility planning in its strategic plans for a few years as part of its DOD Mobility Implementation Plan. As of January 31, 2014, DISA deployed version 1.0 of the unclassified mobility plan, which supports 1800 mobility devices (i.e., iPad, tablets) as well as 80000 BlackBerry phones. The mobility plan itself will be deployed in three phases over 2014, with the first phase focusing on policy, the second phase focusing on security and service, and the third phase focusing on operations and management. There are 16 approved mobile applications with 90 more being vetted for use. All of the current tasks being performed are unclassified, but DISA will continue to work towards a secure mobile solution to enable DOD workers to perform their jobs. Users are being transitioned in according to the priorities set by the commands. DISA also created a Mobility website to track and promote all of its mobility documentation and policies, which include four primary goals listed in Figure 15.

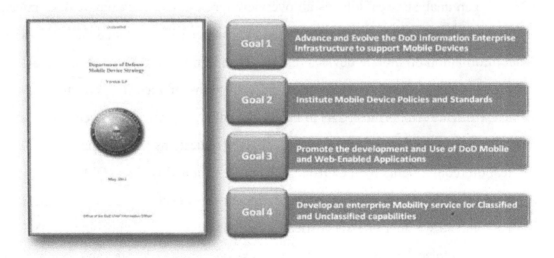

Figure 15.   Mobility goals, DISA (DISA: DOD MOBILITY PROGRAM, 2012.)

The DOD Mobility Implementation Plan pinpoints potential issues in regard to governance, cost management, and mobile device management. Metrics will be taken on mobile device statistics and audits will be performed to ensure the best solutions are being taken. Requirements will be developed for policies including application development, accreditation, and certification. A DOD Mobility Program Management Office (PMO) is being established to handle all mobility related tasking. The General Services Administration (GSA) will be working on a mobile contract that encompasses the entire government's mobility needs. This will include the infrastructure, devices, applications, information assurance and any necessary user training. The BYOD option is not approved at this time but will continue to be evaluated for future use. Classified access will be authorized over encrypted websites only but not through contactless CAC interaction with a mobile device itself.

THIS PAGE INTENTIONALLY LEFT BLANK

LIST OF REFERENCES

Al Hasib, A., & Haque, A. (2008). A comparative study of the performance and security issues of AES and RSA cryptography, in *Third International Conference on Convergence and Hybrid Information Technology* (Busan), Volume 2, 505–510, 10.1109/ICCIT.2008.179

Chatterjee, J., & Gupta, D. (2009). Secure access of smart cards using elliptic curve cryptosystems, in *5th International Conference on Wireless Communications, Networking and Mobile Computing* (Beijing), 4635-4638, 10.1109/WICOM.2009.5302782

Defense Enterprise Mobility – A game changer for the Department of Defense. (2012, Jan.). , DISA: DOD Mobility Program. Retrieved from http://www.disa.mil/Services/Enterprise-Services/Mobility

Dagdelen, O., Fischlin, M., Gagliardoni, T., Marson, G., Mittelbach, A., & Onete, C. (2013). A cryptographic analysis of OPACITY. Retrieved from http://eprint.iacr.org/2013/234.pdf

Department of Defense. (2011). Department of Defense (DoD) Information Technology (IT) enterprise strategy and roadmap. Retrieved from http://dodcio.defense.gov/Portals/0/Documents/Announcement/Signed_ITESR_6 SEP11.pdf

Department of Homeland Security(DHS). (2004, August 27). Policy for a common identification standard for federal employees and contractors (Homeland Security Presidential Directive 12). Washington, DC: George W. Bush.

Effective identity and access management in a mobile world [White Paper] (n.d.). Retrieved August 2014 from https://www1.good.com/forms/good-vault-whitepaper.html

Federal Information Processing Standards (FIPS) Publication 186–4, Digital Signature Standard (DSS). (2013). Retrieved from http://nvlpubs.nist.gov/nistpubs/FIPS/NIST.FIPS.186-4.pdf.

Federal Information Security Management Act (FISMA), Public Law (P.L.) 107–347, NIST special publication 800–157 Guidelines for derived personal identity verification (PIV) credentials. (2014). Retrieved from http://www.nist.gov/publication-portal.cfm.

Information Technology (IT) Enterprise strategy and roadmap. (2011). Retrieved from http://dodcio.defense.gov/Portals/0/Documents/Announcement/Signed_ITESR_6 SEP11.pdf

Mobile devices and identity applications. (2012, Sep.). Retrieved March 2015 from
http://www.smartcardalliance.org/resources/pdf/mobile_identity_brief_082712.pd
f

Nassr, D., Bahig, H., Bhery, A., & Daoud, S., A new RSA vulnerability using continued
fractions, in *IEEE/ACS International Conference on Computer Systems and
Applications* 10.1109/AICCSA.2008.4493604 (Doha, Institute of Electrical and
Electronics Engineers (IEEE), 2008),694–701, 10.1109/AICCSA.2008.4493604

Owor, R., Dajani, K., Okonkwo, Z., & Hamilton, J. (2007). An elliptical cryptographic
algorithm for RF wireless devices, in *Proceedings of the 2007 Winter Simulation
Conference* 1–4244–1306–5 (Washington, D.C.: Institute of Electrical and
Electronics Engineers (IEEE), 2007), 1424–429, 10.1109/WSC.2007.4419752

Takia, T. (Feb 13, 2013). Department of Defense commercial mobile device
implementation plan [Memorandum]. Washington, DC: Department of Defense.
Retrieved from http://www.defense.gov/news/dodcMdimplementationplan.pdf

"The case for elliptic curve cryptography: elliptic curve security and efficiency"
Paragraph 6. (2009, Jan. 15). Retrieved from
https://www.nsa.gov/business/programs/elliptic_curve.shtml

The open protocol for access control identification and ticketing with privacY for secure
contactless transactions and enabling logical and physical access [Powerpoint]
(n.d.). Retrieved August 2014 from
http://www.smartcardalliance.org/resources/pdf/OPACITY_Overview%203.8.pdf

United States Department of Defense (DOD) Common Access Card (CAC): a smart
move to next-generation identity credentials [Brochure] (2010). Retrieved March
2015 from http://www.gemalto.com/brochures-site/download-
site/Documents/dod.pdf

www.ingramcontent.com/pod-product-compliance
Lightning Source LLC
Chambersburg PA
CBHW060445060326
40690CB00019B/4347